TEYNHAM

11. Opening with the line, this small station served only 900 people, although this number nearly doubled during the following three decades. The large goods shed reflected the fact that freight was an important part of revenue here. (Lens of Sutton)

12. The spacious goods shed handled the considerable seasonal traffic from the numerous orchards of the district. The coupled chimney stacks are an interesting architectural feature. (Lens of Sutton)

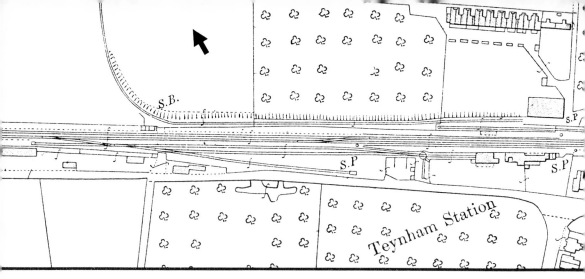

The 1908 edition includes Eastwood's 3ft 6in
tramway curving north to their brickworks.

13. On the right of this view towards London are some of the orchards of Barrow Green and the exchange sidings with Eastwood's grass covered tramway. Narrow gauge wagons and a horse are partly obscurred by two main line wagons, with curved ends. (Lens of Sutton)

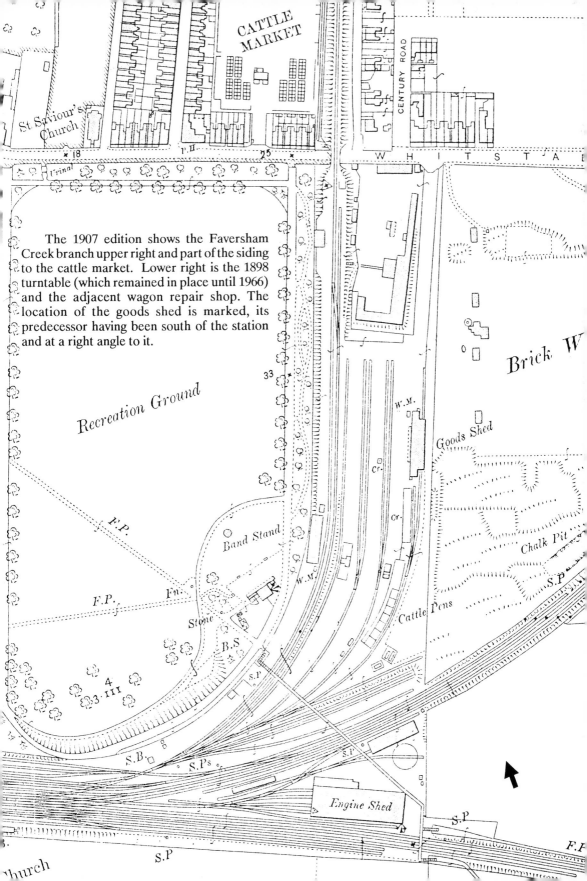

CATTLE
MARKET

CENTURY ROAD

St Saviour's
Church

Urinal

W H I T S T A

18   P.H   35

The 1907 edition shows the Faversham
Creek branch upper right and part of the siding
to the cattle market. Lower right is the 1898
turntable (which remained in place until 1966)
and the adjacent wagon repair shop. The
location of the goods shed is marked, its
predecessor having been south of the station
and at a right angle to it.

Brick W

W.M.

Goods Shed

33

Recreation Ground

Cr.

Chalk Pit

F.P.

Cr.

Band Stand

S.P

W.M.

F.P.   Fn.

Cattle Pens

Stone

B.S

4
3·III

S.P

S.B

S.Ps

Engine Shed   S.P

church   S.P   F.P

24. During the rebuilding of the station, new offices of similar design were provided on both sides of the line and they remained largely unaltered in 1991. This is the downside in the pre-motor age. (D.Cullum coll.)

Working timetable for May 1888.

KENT COAST RAILWAY.
WEEK DAYS—UP.

UP.	1 2 3 C				1 2 3 C		1 2 3 C		1 2 3				1 2 3 C		1 2 3 C	
	arr. a.m.	dep. a.m.			arr. a.m.	dep. a.m.	arr. a.m.	dep. a.m.	arr. a.m.	dep. a.m.			arr. p.m.	dep. p.m.	arr. p.m.	dep. p.m.
Ramsgate	...	8 0	...	...	...	8 37	...	10 0	...	10 10	...	...	...	12 5	...	1 15
Broadstairs	8 6	8 7	...	...	8 40	8 41	10 5	10 6	10 16	10 17	...	...	12 11	12 12	1 20	1 21
East Margate	...	...	...	...	...	...	...	...	10 21	10 22	...	...	...	...	1 26	1 27
Margate	8 13	8 15	...	...	8 47	8 48	10 11	10 13	10 23	10 25	...	...	12 18	12 20	1 28	1 30
Westgate-on-Sea	8 19	8 20	...	...	8 53	8 54	10 16	10 18	10 29	10 30	...	...	12 24	12 25	1 34	1 35
Birchington-on-Sea	8 24	8 25	...	...	8 58	8 59	...	10 20	10 35	...	...	...	12 29	12 30	1 39	1 40
Herne Bay	8 37	8 39	...	...	9 13	9 14	...	10 30	...	...	...	...	12 43	12 45	1 54	1 56
Whitstable	8 46	8 47	...	...	9 22	9 23	...	10 33	...	...	...	...	12 53	12 54	2 4	2 5
Graveney Siding	...	...	...	...	...	...	...	...	...	...	...	...	...	...	...	...
Faversham	...	8 57	...	...	9 34	...	...	10 45	...	...	...	...	1 6	...	2 17	...

UP.	1 2 3		1 2 3				Goods G		1 2 3		1 2 3		1 2 3		Goods. Not on Sats. D	F
	arr. p.m.	dep. p.m.	arr. p.m.	dep. p.m.			arr. p.m.	dep. p.m.	arr. p.m.	dep. p.m.	arr. p.m.	dep. p.m.	arr. p.m.	dep. p.m.	arr. p.m.	dep. p.m.
Ramsgate	...	2 10	...	4 0	...	...	...	...	...	5 45	...	7 5	...	7 30	...	7 20
Broadstairs	2 16	2 17	4 6	4 7	...	...	...	...	5 51	5 52	7 11	7 12	7 35	7 37	7 26	7 45
East Margate	2 22	2 23	...	...	...	...	...	...	5 57	5 58	...	...	...	...	...	...
Margate	2 27	...	4 13	4 15	...	...	...	5 50	6 0	...	7 18	7 20	7 43	7 45	7 53	8 10
Westgate-on-Sea	...	...	4 19	4 20	...	...	5 55	6 25	...	...	7 24	7 25	...	7 48	8 14	8 30
Birchington-on-Sea	...	...	4 24	4 25	...	...	6 35	7 5	...	...	7 29	7 30	...	7 51	8 37	9 0
Herne Bay	...	...	4 38	4 40	...	...	7 20	8 5	...	...	7 44	7 46	8 2	8 3	9 20	9 38
Whitstable	...	...	4 48	4 49	...	...	8 13	8 40	...	...	7 55	7 56	...	8 9	9 50	10 10
Graveney Siding	...	...	...	...	...	...	8 47	8 55	...	...	...	...	...	...	10 20	10 30
Faversham	...	...	5 1	...	...	...	9 5	...	...	...	8 8	...	8 20	...	10 40	...

UP.	1 2 3		1 2 3		1 2 3											
	arr. p.m.	dep. p.m.	arr. p.m.	dep. p.m.	arr. p.m.	dep. p.m.										
Ramsgate	...	8 15	...	9 5	...	10 30	...	...	...	...	...	...	...	...	...	...
Broadstairs	8 21	8 22	9 11	9 12	10 36	10 37	...	...	...	...	...	...	...	...	...	...
East Margate	8 27	8 28	9 17	9 18	...	...	...	...	...	...	...	...	...	...	...	...
Margate	8 30	...	9 19	9 20	10 45	...	...	...	...	...	...	...	...	...	...	...
Westgate-on-Sea	...	...	9 24	9 25	...	...	...	...	...	...	...	...	...	...	...	...
Birchington-on-Sea	...	...	9 30	...	...	...	...	...	...	...	...	...	...	...	...	...
Herne Bay	...	...	...	...	...	...	...	...	...	...	...	...	...	...	...	...
Whitstable	...	...	...	...	...	...	...	...	...	...	...	...	...	...	...	...
Graveney Siding	...	...	...	...	...	...	...	...	...	...	...	...	...	...	...	...
Faversham	...	...	...	...	...	...	...	...	...	...	...	...	...	...	...	...

C These Trains run through to London.

D This Train runs through to Blackfriars, and does not run on Saturdays.

F It is important that this Goods Train should reach Faversham punctually. It shunts at Broadstairs for 7.30 p.m. Up Train.

G This Train to perform all Station Shunting on the Branch, and to work up Trucks to Faversham so as to relieve the 7.20 p.m. Ramsgate Goods.

Engines and Empty Trains will run as required between Ramsgate and Margate.

98. The 5.0 pm up from Ramsgate was the return working of the Pullman Cars to Victoria. Class 5 no. 75065 is dropping at 1 in 264 on 14th June 1959, the goods yard on the right still busy with coal traffic. It closed on 3rd June 1963. (J.J.Smith)

lower left
99. In 1990, the exterior of the down side retained its 1926 features, notably its ornamental belfry. Both flights of steps from street level, parallel to the road bridge, were still in use, although less so since a footbridge was provided between the platforms in the 1970s. (J.Scrace)

100. A southward view in 1990 shows both footbridges and the steelwork of the road bridge in the "six-foot". Part of the former parcels office on the down platform is occupied by the Isle of Thanet Railway Society. The up side buildings were altered and extended in 1937, but suffered bomb damage in WWII. (J.Scrace)

SOUTH OF BROADSTAIRS

101. A typical local train of the late 1930s runs south and approaches the point of divergence of the 1926 deviation from the original LCDR route - see the inset map in the introduction. The H class tanks were particularly successful SECR engines, this example being in use from 1909 until 1963. In 1936, there were over 161,000 passenger bookings between Margate and Ramsgate. (Revd.A.W.V.Mace)

102. Class B1 no. 61188 enters the 20 chain curve at the commencement of the connecting line between the former LCDR and SER routes. The train is the 10.35am from Victoria on 25th May 1953. The old trackbed is on the right and Holy Cross Convent is in the background. (S.C.Nash)

103. The old route to Ramsgate Harbour descended at 1 in 75 for one mile, through the tunnel on the left, while the 1926 line climbs at 1 in 264 to the right, to Dumpton Park. Work is in progress on the construction of a track paralleling hut in readiness for electrification. (British Rail)

THROUGH EXPRESS SERVICE
(Via WILLESDEN and KENSINGTON)
BETWEEN THE
LONDON MIDLAND & SCOTTISH RAILWAY
AND THE
SOUTHERN RAILWAY.

CORRIDOR CARRIAGES.

Restaurant Cars in both directions.

Week Days only.	a.m.
Liverpool (Lime Street) ....dep.	10 30
Manchester (London Road) .... "	10 40
Manchester (Victoria) .... "	9 20
Leeds (New Station) .... "	9 22
Bradford (Exchange) .... "	8§37
Halifax .... "	8 50
Huddersfield .... "	9 50
Rochdale .... "	9 25
Oldham (Clegg Street) .... "	10 12
Buxton .... "	9 30
Stockport .... "	10 50
Kendal .... "	7 41
Carnforth .... "	8 41
Morecambe (Euston Road) .... "	8 35
Lancaster (Castle Station) .... "	8 55
Preston .... "	9 29
Wigan (North Western) .... "	9 56
Warrington (Bank Quay) .... "	10 17
Birkenhead (Woodside) .... "	9 35
Chester .... "	10 32
Crewe .... "	11 46
Stoke-on-Trent .... "	10 55
Shrewsbury .... "	10 15
Stafford .... "	11 50
Nuneaton .... "	1 7
Wolverhampton (High Level) .... "	11 57
Dudley .... "	11 20
	p.m.
Walsall .... "	12 2
Birmingham (New Street) .... "	12 30
Coventry .... "	12 58
Warwick (Milverton) .... "	12 20
Leamington Spa .... "	12 24
Rugby .... "	1 18
Northampton (Castle) .... "	2 0
Willesden Junction .... arr.	3 11
	p.m.
Willesden Junction .... dep.	3 21
Kensington (Addison Road) .... "	3 30
Chatham .... arr.	4 30
Sittingbourne .... "	5§23
Sheerness-on-Sea .... "	6 16
Faversham .... "	5§36
Canterbury East .... "	6 13
Dover Priory .... "	6 50
Whitstable Town .... "	5 6
Herne Bay .... "	5 15
Birchington-on-Sea .... "	5 29
Westgate-on-Sea .... "	5 35
Margate West .... "	5 39
Broadstairs .... "	5 52
Ramsgate Harbour .... "	5 58

Week Days only.		a.m.	a.m.	a.m.
Ramsgate Harbour ....dep.				11 0
Broadstairs .... "	Except Saturdays.	Sats. only.		11 8
Margate West .... "				11 20
Westgate-on-Sea .... "				11 26
Birchington-on-Sea .... "				11 32
Herne Bay .... "				11 46
Whitstable Town .... "				11 56
Dover Priory .... "	9 42	9 50		....
Canterbury East .... "	10 27	10 42		....
Faversham .... "	10 54	11 11		....
Sheerness-on-Sea .... "	10 20	10 13		....
Sittingbourne .... "	11 12	11 30		....
				p.m.
Chatham				12 30
Kensington (Addison Road) .... arr.				1 35
Willesden Junction				1 45
				p.m.
Willesden Junction .... dep.				1 55
Northampton (Castle) .... arr.				4 14
Rugby .... "				4 55
Leamington Spa .... "				5 0
Warwick (Milverton) .... "				4 50
Nuneaton .... "				5 39
Stoke-on-Trent .... "				4 13
Coventry .... "				4 41
Birmingham (New Street) .... "				6 49
Walsall .... "				5 24
Dudley .... "				5 25
Wolverhampton (High Level) .... "				5*48
Stafford .... "				7*35
Shrewsbury .... "				
Crewe .... "				5 26
Chester .... "				6 24
Birkenhead (Woodside) .... "				7 0
Warrington (Bank Quay) .... "				6 29
Wigan (North Western) .... "				7 24
Preston .... "				7 24
Lancaster (Castle Station) .... "				8 1
Morecambe (Euston Road) .... "				8 25
Carnforth .... "				8 23
Kendal .... "				9 5
Stockport .... "				6 12
Buxton .... "				7α25
Oldham (Clegg Street) .... "				7 15
Rochdale .... "				7V49
Huddersfield .... "				8 11
Halifax .... "				‑‑§
Bradford (Exchange) .... "				9 V 6
Leeds (New Station) .... "				9 10
Manchester (Victoria) .... "				7 2
Manchester (London Road) .... "				6 28
Liverpool (Lime Street) .... "				6 35

* Via Birmingham. § Passengers from Halifax cross from Victoria to London Road Station, Manchester, at their own expense. a On Saturdays arrives Buxton 8·33 p.m. β On Saturdays arrives Sittingbourne 5·34 p.m. and Faversham 5·48 p.m. V Via Stockport and Manchester (Victoria).
Passengers from and to Stations shown in Thick Type travel in Through Carriages.
Passengers from and to other Stations change at the appropriate Junction into or out of the Through Carriages.

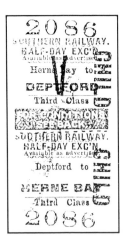

July 1924

MP Middleton Press

Easebourne Lane, Midhurst. West Sussex. GU29 9AZ
(0730) 813169

Write or telephone for our latest booklist

BRANCH LINES

BRANCH LINES TO MIDHURST
BRANCH LINES AROUND MIDHURST
BRANCH LINES TO HORSHAM
BRANCH LINE TO SELSEY
BRANCH LINES TO EAST GRINSTEAD
BRANCH LINES TO ALTON
BRANCH LINE TO HAYLING
BRANCH LINE TO TENTERDEN
BRANCH LINES TO NEWPORT
BRANCH LINES TO TUNBRIDGE WELLS
BRANCH LINE TO SWANAGE
BRANCH LINES TO LONGMOOR
BRANCH LINE TO LYME REGIS
BRANCH LINE TO FAIRFORD
BRANCH LINE TO ALLHALLOWS
BRANCH LINES AROUND ASCOT
BRANCH LINES AROUND WEYMOUTH
BRANCH LINE TO HAWKHURST
BRANCH LINES AROUND EFFINGHAM JN
BRANCH LINE TO MINEHEAD
BRANCH LINE TO SHREWSBURY

SOUTH COAST RAILWAYS

CHICHESTER TO PORTSMOUTH
BRIGHTON TO EASTBOURNE
RYDE TO VENTNOR
EASTBOURNE TO HASTINGS
PORTSMOUTH TO SOUTHAMPTON
HASTINGS TO ASHFORD
SOUTHAMPTON TO BOURNEMOUTH
ASHFORD TO DOVER
BOURNEMOUTH TO WEYMOUTH
DOVER TO RAMSGATE

SOUTHERN MAIN LINES

HAYWARDS HEATH TO SEAFORD
EPSOM TO HORSHAM
CRAWLEY TO LITTLEHAMPTON
THREE BRIDGES TO BRIGHTON
WATERLOO TO WOKING
VICTORIA TO EAST CROYDON
EAST CROYDON TO THREE BRIDGES
WOKING TO SOUTHAMPTON
WATERLOO TO WINDSOR
LONDON BRIDGE TO EAST CROYDON
BASINGSTOKE TO SALISBURY
SITTINGBOURNE TO RAMSGATE

COUNTRY RAILWAY ROUTES

BOURNEMOUTH TO EVERCREECH JN
READING TO GUILDFORD
WOKING TO ALTON
BATH TO EVERCREECH JUNCTION
GUILDFORD TO REDHILL
EAST KENT LIGHT RAILWAY
FAREHAM TO SALISBURY
BURNHAM TO EVERCREECH JUNCTION
REDHILL TO ASHFORD
YEOVIL TO DORCHESTER
ANDOVER TO SOUTHAMPTON

LONDON SUBURBAN RAILWAYS

CHARING CROSS TO DARTFORD
HOLBORN VIADUCT TO LEWISHAM
KINGSTON & HOUNSLOW LOOPS
CRYSTAL PALACE AND CATFORD LOOP

STEAMING THROUGH

STEAMING THROUGH EAST HANTS
STEAMING THROUGH SURREY
STEAMING THROUGH WEST SUSSEX
STEAMING THROUGH THE ISLE OF WIGHT
STEAMING THROUGH WEST HANTS

OTHER RAILWAY BOOKS

GARRAWAY FATHER & SON
LONDON CHATHAM & DOVER RAILWAY
INDUSTRIAL RAILWAYS OF THE S. EAST
WEST SUSSEX RAILWAYS IN THE 1980s
SOUTH EASTERN RAILWAY

OTHER BOOKS

WALKS IN THE WESTERN HIGH WEALD
TILLINGBOURNE BUS STORY

MILITARY DEFENCE OF WEST SUSSEX
BATTLE OVER SUSSEX 1940

SURREY WATERWAYS
KENT AND EAST SUSSEX WATERWAYS
HAMPSHIRE WATERWAYS